bolder

STEPPING OUT BY STEPPING INTO GOD'S WORD

AMANDA BEDZRAH

EVELYN HOUSE PUBLISHING

BOLDER

Stepping Out by Stepping into God's Word

Cover Design – Evelyn House Publishing

Editor – Wendy H Jones

ISBN: 978-1-8383044-2-3

Evelyn House Publishing

Printed in the United Kingdom

contents

Foreword	vii
Acknowledgments	xi
Introduction	xiii
How To Use this Devotional	xv
SPIRIT TO SPIRIT	1
TAKE COURAGE	3
STEADFAST HEART	6
WITH JESUS	9
THE GOOD SHEPHERD	12
SOFT IS STRONG	16
POWER OF WORDS	20
THE AUDACITY OF JACOB	22
THE UNWANTED MIRACLE?	26
WE ARE WORTHY	30
GOD'S CHILD	34
A SIMPLE TASK	37
SPEAK UP FOR YOUR BLESSING	41
GOOD OR GOD?	45
REJECTION OR REDIRECTION?	49
GRATEFUL ALWAYS	53
REST TO RECHARGE	57
ALONE IS TOO MUCH	61
THE HEART OF A CENTURION	64
FREEDOM IN CHRIST	67
THE THRONE OF GOD	70
LET GO AND FORGIVE	73
BE A BLESSING	77
STORMS OF LIFE!	80
THE ART OF PRAYING SCRIPTURE	84
PRAYING SCRIPTURE - 1	88
PRAYING SCRIPTURE - 2	90
PRAYING SCRIPTURE - 3	93
PRAYING SCRIPTURE - 4	96

THE PRAYING SCRIPTURE ALARM - 5 99
PRAYING PRAYERS FROM THE BIBLE - 6 102

End Note 105
OTHER BOOKS BY AMANDA BEDZRAH 107
About the Author 109

For my daughter Remeny.

Know that you have no limitations. You can do more and be more with Christ Jesus.

foreword

> "After they prayed, the place where they were meeting was shaken. And they were all filled with the Holy Spirit and spoke the word of God boldly". Acts 4:31

The woman that you will be one month from now really needs you to read this book.

If you like a devotional to comfort you, lay this book aside. If you want a devotional to resemble a warm, enfolding bubble bath, then this is not the devotional for you. But if you are longing to be changed and you are longing to grow, if you are crying out to be a disciple rather than a follower, if your heart is to strap on your armour, pick up your sword and be a kingdom carrier then carry on reading.

I did not expect this 31-day devotional to make my mind, heart and spirit work so hard!

What does it mean to be bold? Is bold different to brave? Which part of me is bold, which part of me needs to be bolder? Which part of me, small and tucked away, doesn't feel bold at all? If I were bolder in Him what would it look like and feel like?

I picked up this book knowing I wanted to be bolder for God. I wanted more 'holy bold' in my life. I know Amanda well, so I expected her to deliver some good teaching and some useful tools. She did. What I did not expect was that the power of His word and Amanda's challenging wisdom would start a transforming work in me.

There are scriptures, reflections, helpful tips, and prayers. But it was the BOLDer statements at the end of most days that somehow got rooted in me. Some have now become daily declarations for me:

- I am bold because I have been with Jesus.
- I am bold because I embrace all of my emotions, even my tears.
- I am bold because I am not afraid to be rejected, I know that God always has a great plan for my life.
- I am bold because I am not ashamed to speak up for my blessings.

Amanda is wife, mother to three, ordained minister, NHS Associate Director, CEO of Empower a Woman a Non-Profit organisation, and she volunteers with the Bible Society. Her fruitfulness is astonishing and sometimes exhausting! But her early life did not so position her, rather she has pursued the Lord with passion and desire, grasped the truths of the Word and refused to let them go until she has seen transformation in her identity and in her thinking, she has truly and authentically walked this journey from trauma to holy boldness.

She is a living testimony of one of her BOLDer Statements:

- I am bold because I hold firmly to the word of God, refusing to let go until it transforms my life.

Dear Reader, the BOLDER Woman you will be one month from now really needs you to read this book.

Carol Bostock
Beauty From Ashes
Healing and Hope for the Hurting www.beautyfromashes.co.uk

acknowledgments

I am extremely grateful to the Almighty God for His blessing, His grace, His strength, and this awesome gift He has blessed me with. It does not come without its trials but at every step of the journey, He is consistently with me, leading, guiding and directing me. My life is completely dedicated to the service of God.

To my husband – Thank you for loving me and encouraging me to be the woman God has called me to be. Your constant support is in words and action and I am eternally grateful. I thank God for creating you for me. I know it cannot be easy to be married to a woman like me, but you do it so well.

To my children – Thank you for loving me and giving me the time I need to research and write. Thank you for enduring many junk food days when I was too immersed in writing to cook (I am sure you enjoyed them though ;). You three are truly a gift from God.

To my parents – You laid a solid foundation of love and prayers and named me JOY. I thank you for blessing me with such a prophetic name. I pray to live out my life being a joy to this world.

To my sisters – You are truly my best friends and my biggest cheerleaders. Thank you for being there always to love, and encourage me, even when I'm being a naughty baby sister.

To my mentors – I am so grateful for your constant prayers, words of encouragement and intercession. Thank you for leading with grace and teaching me to grow into the woman God has called me to be.

I am also thankful to my girlfriends who are very dear to me. I am so blessed to have such great women who encourage me and excuse my silence in the seasons of writing. It is a pleasure to do life with you all.

A massive thank you to everyone who buys and reads this book, and to those who buy my books and gift it to others. Without you all, my writing will have no meaning or purpose. I am truly grateful to you.

introduction

Have you ever wanted to step out into the world with confidence but found yourself unable to do so? Does your heart long to do more for God, but somehow you can't find the courage? Do you watch with envy and anxiety as you see others live your dreams and wish you could be just like them?

I know exactly how you feel because I have walked in those shoes. For many years, I was imprisoned by fear, shame, low self-esteem and insecurity, and I felt unable to live my life to its fullest. It is frustrating knowing God has called you to a great life but finding neither the courage nor the strength to live it.

Don't get me wrong, we all have some measure of boldness. We fully show up sometimes and do what is necessary every day. But what if you could be bolder? What if you could show up consistently and make boldness a lifestyle? I truly believe there is power in the word of God to enable us to constantly live confident lives.

At the word of Jesus, Peter stepped out of the boat to do what was impossible for man to do – he walked on water (see Matthew 14:22-33). What would you do if you were bolder? Think about it for a minute; be honest with yourself as you imagine life without fear.

The truth is, with your eyes fixed on Jesus and His word, you can do anything He calls you to do.

When God speaks, the impossible becomes possible. His Word has the power to make you more courageous, more daring and more confident in faith. God's word is true, you can trust in and rely on it. No journey to transformation is without opposition from the enemy, so prepare to be challenged, but know that God is on your side as am I. This is why I must pray for you. As you are being transformed by the word of God, I will pray straight from the word of God. This is one of my favourite prayers which comes from the word of God. It blesses my heart so much, and I know it will bless yours.

"I pray that out of His glorious riches He may strengthen you with power through His Spirit in your inner being, so that Christ may dwell in your hearts through faith. And I pray that you, being rooted and established in love, may have power, together with all the Lord's holy people, to grasp how wide and long and high and deep is the love of Christ, and to know this love that surpasses knowledge—that you may be filled to the measure of all the fullness of God." In Jesus name. Amen. (**Ephesians 3:16-20)**

This 31-day devotional will transform your life, using a scripture-based approach to empower you to become bolder. Are you ready to step out with greater boldness by stepping into God's word? Then join me on this 31-day journey.

how to use this devotional

- Read the scripture out loud and meditate on the words.
- Read the exhortation for the day and make notes in a dedicated journal.
- Speak out the BOLDer statement.
- Pray the short prayer at the end.

spirit to spirit

DAY 1

"The Lord be with your spirit. Grace be with you all." 2 Timothy 4:22

The first time I came across the verse above, my heart immediately leapt within me. It was an awesome moment. What a prayer! What a blessing! It's the perfect way to end a greeting.

The word in this verse is powerful – ***The Lord be with your spirit.*** Take a moment to ponder on this. Did you know God wants to go beyond our minds, our souls, our bodies and even our circumstances straight into our spirits? Yes, He wants to. How does this make you feel? Write how you feel in your journal. For me, knowing that God is with my spirit fills me with overflowing joy and confidence. That knowledge puts a bounce in my step and makes me feel complete. Receive Him today and let this truth fill you with courage.

The Bible tells us in John 4:24 that ***"God is spirit, and His worshipers must worship in Spirit and in truth."*** The spirit of the Lord is with you, and His grace is upon you. This is a spirit-to-spirit encounter, a relationship much deeper than you could ever think or imagine.

He is with you. He is for you. No one can be against you. Stand tall.

True boldness starts from knowing who you are in Jesus and taking hold of His word. The opening verse teaches us God is with our spirit – the very core of who we are, and His grace is present. As you start this journey to being bolder, let this truth be a solid foundation for you. According to His word, He is with you, and He is for you. You are not alone on this journey. The Holy Spirit will walk with you as a guide, a helper, a comforter, and a healer. He will be exactly what He needs to be for you in this season. Stand firm and enjoy the journey with Him.

BOLDer Statement

I am bold because the Spirit of God is with me and is in me.

PRAYER

Dear Lord,

I thank you for your Word, which is true. I pray that You, Lord, will be with my spirit and Your grace will be with me. As I travel this journey to becoming a bolder version of myself, I know that You are with me, and that already gives me courage. I ask that You prepare my heart and mind to receive all that You have in store for me. In Jesus' name. Amen

---

take courage

DAY 2

> "But you, take courage! Do not let your hands be weak, for your work shall be rewarded." 2 Chronicles 15:7

I have a vivid imagination, which makes reading the Bible interesting. When I think of today's verse, I imagine standing in a beautiful field with lots of trees and flowers with birds singing. I hear the gentle trickle of water from the river beside me. In front of me is Jesus, a serious yet gentle look on His face. He is gazing at me and smiling. His hand is outstretched towards me, and in His open right palm is a huge measure of courage, and He is saying to me – But you, TAKE COURAGE.

I stand there, looking at my saviour, in awe of Him, aware I have two choices – take it or leave it. I choose to take courage. As I receive it by faith, I feel bolder and stronger. Then I look at my hands and say to myself, "I will not let these hands be weak. I have taken courage."

The Lord sent His prophet Azariah to King Asa at a time when Judah and Benjamin were in great distress. They were worshipping false gods and had turned their backs on the one true God. When Azariah arrived and spoke God's word to the King, the bible tells us King Asa took courage, removed all the false Gods, repaired God's altar and turned the nations back to God, bringing sacrifice and praise. They sought the Lord and they found Him. How awesome is that? Praise God.

When the disciples saw Jesus walking on water, they were afraid. They thought He was a ghost. Immediately, Jesus told them, "Take courage; it is I. Do not be afraid." Filled with courage, Peter was bold enough to step out of the boat and walk on water (Matthew 14:26-28). What amazing things could you accomplish if you took courage? God's Word says it is yours for the taking. You could walk on water like Peter did if you stepped out of the boat with your eyes fixed on Jesus. He is the one who calls you to come to Him, and He is giving you a personal invitation today. He wants you to grasp something that can make you bold. He says, "TAKE COURAGE." Will you answer His call? I believe you will. I can see you reaching out your hand to take courage in Jesus' name.

Courage will enable you to achieve more than you ever dreamed of. When you have courage, you will overcome fear and weakness. You will be equipped to fulfil God's purpose for your life and receive His rewards.

So, I ask you once more, will you take courage? See, Jesus is stretching out His right hand to you today; all you need to do is reach out in faith and take it. As you do, you will sense a new boldness in your spirit.

BOLDer Statement

I am bold because the Lord has given me courage and I have taken it.

PRAYER

Dear Lord,

I thank you for your loving care and attention. Help me to accept the gift of courage, strengthen my hands that they will not be feeble. I thank you for your promise of rewards. In Jesus' name, Amen.

---

steadfast heart

DAY 3

"They will have no fear of bad news; their hearts are steadfast, trusting in the LORD." Psalm 112:7

One summer afternoon in 2013, my husband went to the grocery store. A few hours after he had been gone, I called his phone. It was switched off. I tried again and again but no answer. A wave of panic washed over me, and I started to sweat and pace the room. I imagined the worst scenarios, from a minor accident to death. I expected a knock on the door from the police any minute. I was in a state of frenzy in my bedroom, unable to calm down. I tried calling one more time, and then I broke down in tears.

I finally went downstairs, and he was in the kitchen putting away the groceries. I had been so absorbed in my own fears that I did not hear the door open or even think to check if he was back home. I took one look at him, and anger surged through me. "Where is your phone?" I yelled. He looked at me, puzzled. He was calm, busy, oblivious to my distress. With his head still in the fridge, he said, "It's upstairs. I left it to charge. I switched it off so it would charge faster." Then he closed the fridge, looked at me, and asked, "Why?" I turned around and walked away, feeling foolish. How could I explain to him that for the last several minutes I thought he was seriously injured or dead?

This was not an isolated incident where anxiety had captured me, but it was the incident God used to show me something was seriously wrong, and I turned to him to start a healing work in me. I didn't know there was a kind of fear that held me captive – the fear of bad news. God showed me how much it was limiting my life as I was the reason that I didn't do certain things.

Does the fear of bad news hold you captive? Does it prevent you from being bolder? It is an unusual type of fear, the kind that grips you tightly, feeling like a comfort blanket, but the truth is, fear is a liar.

God wants us to live a life that is bold and fearless. Fear is triggered when we look inwards instead of upwards. We often view life through the lens of our human limitations. No wonder we are often afraid. We truly don't have what it takes by ourselves. Looking inward will lead to fear, which is why God tells us in Proverbs 3:5 to trust in Him with all our hearts.

So, what is the remedy? This verse teaches us that a steadfast heart, one that trusts God, will have no fear of bad news because our trust is not in us or our limitations but in the Lord, who has no limitations.

This verse doesn't mean bad things won't happen. We live in a fallen world, but we can choose to live a victorious life trusting in God with a steadfast heart instead of allowing the fear of bad news to prevent us from stepping out boldly.

BOLDer Statement

I am bold because I am not afraid of bad news. God protects me and all those I love.

PRAYER

Dear Lord,

I pray that You bless me with a steadfast heart, and that I will trust in You completely, living life fearlessly. In Jesus' name, Amen.

---

with jesus

DAY 4

"When they saw the courage of Peter and John and realised that they were unschooled, ordinary men, they were astonished and they took note that these men had been with Jesus." Acts 4:13

You may have heard the following statement before: God does not call the equipped; He equips those He calls. It is a common saying among many preachers. While it may sound like a cliché, it is true. When God calls you to do anything for Him, He does it because of what He knows about you and not what you know about yourself. And there are ample examples in the scriptures. Here are two of them:

- When God called Abraham the father of many nations, he didn't even have a son, yet, Abraham believed Him. (Genesis 17).
- When God called Gideon a mighty warrior, he had not even fought one battle; after a few confirmation

requests from Gideon which God lovingly obliged, he finally believed God. (Judges 6).

These examples prove that the distance between who you are and who God has called you to be is time, faith and trust. Whether you have the faith of Abraham or you need a bit more convincing like Gideon, know you are equipped to do what God has called you to do. Listen to and obey God. Lean on Him, learn from Him, and He will equip you with everything you need to become all He has called you to be.

As you can see from today's scripture, being bolder is not about your knowledge, expertise or experience. It is not even about what you have or don't have. It has very little to do with you but everything to do with Jesus.

For many years, I struggled with the need to prove myself worthy of the call God had placed on my life. I thought I needed theological and academic qualifications to prove myself worthy to teach the word of God. Yet, every time I tried to seek man-given accreditation , I faced numerous obstacles, and it depressed me. One day, God opened my eyes to this scripture. Gently, he reminded me that the only qualification I needed that truly mattered was this one thing – I have been with Jesus. Since then, I have soaked myself in Him and I continue to do so. It does not mean I will not pursue further theological studies; it just means my motive will be right, and it will be done in God's timing.

When God called me, He put in me everything I needed to fulfil that calling. The Bible says I have the Holy Spirit in me who teaches me all things (John 14:26). It is Him who pours in and then I pour out. Every book I have written, including this one, and every message I have preached have been products of this pouring in and out. Whatever study I choose to do will be for my knowledge and personal growth, not because that is what God needs to fulfil His call on my life. If He can use unschooled, ordinary men like Peter and John to radically transform His church and write His word, then He can certainly use you and me.

One of the quickest and most effective ways to become bolder is to be with Jesus. Spend time in His word, in prayer and with thanksgiving. It is the presence of Jesus in your life that will cause people to ***be astonished.*** They will wonder at how great you are, how well you speak, how much confidence you carry; all of this is possible through – BEING WITH JESUS.

Only Jesus makes the difference. Lean on Him.

BOLDer Statement

I am bold because I have been with Jesus.

PRAYER

Dear Jesus,

I am who I am because of who You are. Teach me to be constantly found in You, to lean on, trust in, and learn from You. Open my ears to hear You clearly and give me the grace to obey Your every command. By myself, I am ordinary, but with You I become extraordinary. Thank You that my life will cause people to be astonished. May I never forget that You make the difference in my life. In Jesus' name, Amen.

---

the good shepherd

DAY 5

"The Lord is my shepherd, I lack nothing" Psalm 23:1

I have always loved Psalm 23. We had to learn it by heart in Sunday school. However, I have started to understand and appreciate its truth much more as I mature in Jesus. One day, I sat down to focus on Psalm 23:1. As I pondered on the verse, I found myself wondering what a shepherd actually does. We often read the scripture and take the words at face value, but what if we dug deeper to appreciate its true meaning by putting the words into context? Why did David choose to describe God as a Shepherd?

To understand, I felt the need to know who a shepherd was and what a shepherd did. I read various websites and articles and was fascinated. Not only is shepherding a full-time job, but it's also an intimate one requiring love, patience and total dedication.

Here are the few nuggets I found:

1. A shepherd's primary responsibility is the safety and welfare of the flock. This means many shepherds must be on call for their animals around the clock.
2. A shepherd is responsible for the health and well-being of their flock and for ensuring they are fed and watered.
3. Some shepherds have been known to feed baby lambs with milk bottles when they are unable to nurse by themselves.

I could go on and on as there are so many wonderful things to say about a shepherd. That's why it is even more wonderful that God is our shepherd and a good one at that. We can take comfort in the fact we LACK NOTHING. I don't know about you, but there is something in this word that makes me want to throw my shoulders back, raise my chest in defiant confidence and breathe with a blessed assurance that all is well.

As children of God, we can dwell on this one truth – because we have Jesus, we have everything we need. The Bible teaches us we do not need to worry as we have seen the evidence of God's power to provide for His children. From the parting of the Red Sea to the resurrection of Jesus, we can testify the Almighty God is powerful.

- We serve a God who clothes the lilies (Matthew 6:28).
- We serve a God who sent a bird to feed Elijah (1 Kings 17:6).
- We serve a God who raised a man who was dead for days (John 11:43).
- We serve a God who rained manna from heaven (Exodus 16:4).

- We serve a God who brought water out of a rock. (Numbers 20:11).
- We serve a God who heals the blind and mute (Matthew 12:22).
- We serve a God who fed 5000 men with a little boy's lunch (John 6:9).
- We serve a God who loves us so much He sent His son to die for us (John 3:16).
- We serve a God who sees us (Genesis 16:13).

Our God will do anything to protect His flock. David, who wrote this psalm, fully understood the love and responsibility of a shepherd. He had killed a lion and a bear just to protect his flock. What won't God do to protect us? Jesus himself confirms the word of the Psalmist and tells us He is not just any kind of shepherd but the good shepherd (John 10:11). I pray you rest in this powerful revelation of who Jesus is and it fills you with boldness.

Today as we meditate on this scripture, be reminded we are protected by the Almighty God.

BOLDer STATEMENT

I am bold because God is my Shepherd, and I have everything I need.

PRAYER

Dear Lord,

Thank You for being a good shepherd who looks after me. I trust in Your word, and I believe it is true. You are the all-powerful God, and I praise Your holy name. Thank You for looking after me and all that concerns me. I pray that according to Your will, Your blessings will be made evident in my life so I can be a blessing to others in return. In Jesus' name, Amen.

---

soft is strong

DAY 6

"Jesus wept." John 11:35

I love today's verse. It is short and simple, yet packed full of meaning. I'd encourage you to read the whole of John 11 to put it into proper context. However, here's a summary – Lazarus, his dear friend, was sick. Lazarus died. Jesus turned up four days after his death, wept and still resurrected him. It is a fascinating part of scripture, one that can leave us with many questions. For me, I have found myself asking why Jesus wept over a situation He knew He had the power to change and subsequently did. What was the reason for His tears?

The more I ponder on this passage, the more I realise our emotions are valid – every single one of them. Being bold is not about hiding the truth of how we feel; it's about recognising, embracing, and sharing those feelings and refusing to be limited by them.

Jesus loved Lazarus. He was sad to see his friends and family grieving a loss. It didn't matter that the situation was going to be reversed. Jesus still expressed His grief, demonstrating His compassionate heart and His humanness in difficult circumstances.

As I meditated on this scripture, God revealed three things to me that I would love to share with you.

- God showed me that love, sympathy and compassion for His people move Him to tears. He comes down to experience every emotion we feel; He is not so distant that He's not present with us. When we hurt, He hurts too.
- God wants to remind us that He is grieving with us. He is not sitting in heaven watching all the chaos on earth and smiling. He is not asleep. He is not occupied with other things. He is here with us in the middle of this storm, and He weeps at what is going on right now.
- He also wants us to know that He has resurrection and restoration power. The story doesn't end with Jesus weeping; He went on to raise Lazarus from the dead.

I truly believe God is looking down from heaven with compassion and willing to meet us right where we are, whatever emotion we are experiencing. Tell Him, pour your heart out to Him, and cast all your cares and burdens on Him in exchange for rest.

I don't know about you, but there is something comforting and, at the same time, powerful in knowing Jesus wept. The mental image of Him grieving with me right now fills me with hope.

Tears are a valid and important response to life's challenges, even those that can be changed through prayer. Don't ever be afraid or ashamed to cry. We serve a compassionate God, one who recognises the need for an emotional response to the trials in life. Jesus wept twice in the bible and both times were evidence of His tender heart towards us.

God sees and recognises our tears; they are so precious to Him that He even keeps them. I love the image that Psalm 56:8 portrays, especially the NLT version. It says, "You keep track of all my sorrows. You have collected all my tears in Your bottle. You have recorded each one in Your book." It is difficult to read this verse without getting emotional as it shows us a Father's heart that is tender, one you feel safe to be vulnerable with. Even our tears are not wasted with God. Regardless of what situation has caused them, all our sorrows matter to God.

Today's verse teaches us a simple message – it is okay to cry. Crying is not a sign of weakness or evidence of a lack of faith. Because of the presence of Jesus, we can weep freely and know it is just for the night as the Bible tells us joy is coming in the morning (Psalm 30:5).

We do not weep excessively like those who have no hope or comfort. We can weep knowing we serve a God who responds to the cause of our sorrow. He changes situations. God will take your mess and turn it into a message. God will take your pain and turn it into purpose. The Bible shows us He gives beauty for ashes, the oil of gladness for mourning, and binds up the brokenhearted (Isaiah 61:1-3). Jesus did not leave us as orphans; instead, He left the Holy Spirit with us to be our comforter.

BOLDer Statement

I am bold because I embrace all of my emotions, even my tears.

PRAYER

Dear Father,

Thank You that You care about everything that concerns me, even those things that make me weep. You teach me through Your word it is okay to cry, and when life brings me to my knees with tears, You are always there, waiting to heal and comfort me. Thank You for caring for me so deeply. Thank You for being a place of safety and comfort. In Jesus' name, Amen.

---

power of words

DAY 7

"Gracious words are a honeycomb, sweet to the soul and healing to the bones." Proverbs 16:241

My dear friend Rachel gave me a beautiful plant for Christmas. As much as I love plants, I have been known to kill them long before their time, so much so that my husband once decided to get me a cactus. "You can't kill this one," he said. Guess what? I did!

It's a combination of things: either I water it too much or not at all, or I give it insufficient sunlight – something always goes wrong. However, I was determined to look after my beautiful Red Poinsettia.

Beyond watering the plant, I started speaking to it. Even when the leaves were turning, I would call them beautiful and whisper tenderly to the plant. I thought I was mad, but week by week, I watched that plant blossom and grow. Even the bruised leaves hung on, and I'm happy to say the plant survived until a few weeks ago. Over 4 months? That's a personal record. The plant withered only whilst I was away in

Greece for a week. I'm convinced if I was around and speaking to it daily, it would have survived.

Words are powerful. We have heard that said so many times. In the Bible, many scriptures tell us about the power of words and how they can affect our lives and the lives of others.

- We know life and death are in the tongue.
- We know words are creative and prophetic.
- We know words can build up and tear down.

So, let us speak well. Speak kindly to yourself, about yourself and to others. We are what we speak, and our words can make our souls and bodies thrive or wither. If kind words can keep a plant alive, imagine what they can do for a human soul and body. Think about it and always speak words that give life.

BOLDer Statement

I am bold, so I will speak words that are sweet to the soul and bring health to my body and others.

PRAYER

Dear Lord,

Your Word says the tongue is hard to tame, yet I know I can come to You for help. Today, I pray the words of the Psalmists and ask that You "Set a guard, O LORD, over my mouth; Keep watch over the door of my lips." (Psalm 141:3 NKJV) In Jesus' name, Amen.

---

the audacity of jacob

DAY 8

"Then the man said, "Let me go, for it is daybreak."
But Jacob replied, "I will not let you go unless you bless me." Genesis 32:26

I love Jacob who is also known as Israel. He's one of the men I look forward to meeting in Heaven. David first though; he's my man. But we cannot talk about boldness without talking about Jacob; he was bold!

I had a light bulb moment when I was listening to a message on Jacob. It was from a familiar part of the Bible. I remember spending a lot of time in Genesis, reading all about Jacob, Leah and Rachel, when I was writing my first Bible fiction novel, Leah. But even then, I didn't get the revelation I got from that sermon.

The message was about Jacob wrestling with God. It was good. As the preacher read the scripture, my mind was arrested by a key point, which forced me to go back and read that passage of scripture all over again. It was then I learned the lessons I want to share with you.

The Bible account is in Genesis 32:22-32. However, today's verse is the one that made me stop, think and share. As I read the verse, I wondered: what would have happened if Jacob had just let go? He must have been tired after wrestling all night. At the time this happened, Jacob was an old man. He knew he was wrestling with someone powerful, someone in authority he should have listened to, but he held fast in disobedience, refused to let go and then had the audacity to ask for a blessing. Wow!

I use the word audacity because of the way the Bible describes Jacob - a liar, a swindler, and a deceiver. On the face of it, he didn't look like a likely candidate for blessings at all, yet Jacob knew something we should all know - God does not judge us by our past, and we have a right as children of God to be blessed.

So, here are three lessons I've learnt from this part of scripture:

- Don't be so distracted by what God allows to happen that you take your eyes away from God – Jacob wrestled with an Angel who dislocated his hip - ouch! Yet, Jacob held on and refused to let go. He was resilient. He was not focused on what was happening but on the person he was with. Jacob didn't let a broken hip prevent him from pursuing God. What are you letting stop you? A broken marriage? A broken home? Poor finances or health? No matter what it is, don't let your circumstances be bigger than your God. Nothing you go through surprises Him, even the things our humanness causes to happen. We serve a faithful God who can turn things around. Consider Job. He went through turmoil but held on to God and reaped a just reward. Stay focused.

- He wasn't limited by his past mistakes. He realised he was in the presence of God and asked for a blessing. Relentlessly. Persistently. Jacob didn't stop to think about all the things that disqualified him. He was bold, audacious and fearless in asking God for what he wanted. But the message I love most as a takeaway from this is that God is always willing and waiting with arms wide open to accept us as we are. However, He does not leave us as we are. We see this with Jacob who received a name change to Israel in this battle. Who knows, there may be a name change in store for you. It may not be your name, i.e., Amanda to Sarah. It may be a change from broke to rich, Miss to Mrs, barren to fertile, sick to healed, broken to whole. There is so much God is willing to do if you just take your eyes off your circumstances and focus on Him.

- Jacob didn't let go – what if he listened to the Angel and said, "Oh! God says let go" and he let go? There would have been no blessing. There would have been no name change. The wrestling would have ended there and then. There is power in persistent prayer. Your blessing may be tied to something you release prematurely. Don't let go! Don't give up the good fight of faith. Keep praying. Keep pressing.

There's a blessing on the other side of holding firmly on to God, knowing that regardless of what we've done, we can hold on to God and ask for that blessing. It is our right as children of God to be blessed.

BOLDer Statement

I am bold because I hold firmly to the word of God, refusing to let go until it transforms my life.

PRAYER

Dear Lord,

I thank You for Your word that teaches me to be resilient and to hold firm. Fill me with the boldness to remain rooted in You, knowing my past mistakes do not disqualify me from Your blessings. Thank You for Your unshakeable love. Help me to not give up the good fight of faith and to remain persistent in Your presence through the word and prayer. In Jesus' name, Amen.

---

the unwanted miracle?

DAY 9

"When Jesus saw him lying there and knew that he had already been there a long time, he said to him, "Do you want to be healed?" John 5:6

One night in 2022, I had a dream. There was a blind man who had been blind for many years. He had his family around him who did everything for him. He lay in bed, unable or perhaps unwilling to do much for himself.

Then, I saw a little boy, no more than eight years old. He came and prayed for this man to receive his sight. People stopped to watch, the man's family gathered around him, and this young boy's prayer was answered. The man seemed to receive his healing. As I watched, I knew he had been healed.

However, the next thing I saw was a set of ladders being laid out, as though there was a requirement to test the healing. Would this man climb the ladder without help? I watched with anticipation, wanting the crowd to see this man do what he had never done before and eager for the crowd to cheer and praise God. I wanted to see his family jump with joy and for this to be a conversion story that filled people with faith in and praise to God.

I was shocked when I saw the man, who I knew had been healed, fall flat on his face as though he could not see. All I remember before I woke up was the look on the little boy's face and the taste of disappointment. I woke up confused and perplexed.

I had not even started to ponder what it all meant when suddenly a question dropped in my heart: "Do you want to be healed?" It was like a light bulb went on as I suddenly remembered the Bible story and realised what happened in my dream.

I remember being fascinated by that question many years ago. Jesus asked the crippled man who had stayed many years by the pool of Bethesda that question (John 5:1-14).

To me, it seemed a pointless question. Why would anyone not want to be healed? However, as I began to dig deep, allowing God to unpack that scripture, I understood the reason for the question and a painful truth: not everyone wants to be healed. Why? Well, healing can come with new responsibilities that some people are unwilling to embrace. If you have been bound for many years, freedom usually comes with a price; for some, that might be too costly.

We see this with the Israelites; they were willing to go back to slavery in Egypt instead of changing their lifestyle to one that obeyed God. They did not even trust God and didn't fight to possess the land. Why work hard when slavery is easier? I read a book about some prisoners choosing to re-offend so they could go back to three meals and a roof over their heads instead of being homeless outside prison, or having to work to support themselves. It's a negative mentality but a reality for many.

The man by the pool had benefited from the generosity of strangers for 37 years. He didn't need to find food, work, or do much but lie there and exist. Jesus was right to ask him that question. Having lived that life for so long, was he willing to change? Did he want a change? Because once his healing happens, he goes from being cared for by others to having to care for himself. Now he needs a job, a home, and money for bills - things he never had to consider before.

This brings me back to my dream. I realised the blind man also had to contemplate the impact of his healing. He couldn't stay idle, relying on others for help, any longer. For him, this was an unwanted miracle. He did not want to be healed.

It is not an easy place to be, I know. I've been there. I have experienced the power of God's healing and had to let go of the brokenness I used as a crutch. You don't know how much you love having an excuse for idleness or bad behaviour until it gets taken away. You think you hate bondage until you are faced with the responsibility of freedom.

Jesus changes your heart, but you need to do the work to change your character and take the time to renew your mind. It's not easy, but it's possible with God. There is greater freedom, which can be long-lasting when we take the time to embrace the responsibility of freedom instead of hiding behind the familiarity of shackles that feel comfortable.

Don't be afraid to step out in faith, to do something new, to embrace a healing that will lead to a different lifestyle. Do not be afraid of change or to change. Don't be afraid to be healed. Don't be afraid to seek freedom from the things that hold you bound. God wants to heal, restore, and redeem you. Yes, healing comes at a price, but it also comes with a reward that far outweighs the cost.

BOLDer Statement

I am bold. I will not let fear stop me from being made whole in Christ Jesus.

PRAYER

Dear Lord,

Yes, I open my mind and declare – Lord, I want to be healed. I trust my life in Your hands. I ask You to deliver me from anything that seeks to hold me captive and prevent me from living the life You have destined for me. I pray for the courage to step out in faith and walk in the freedom that You died for me to have. In Jesus' name, Amen.

---

we are worthy

DAY 10

"But the Lord God called to the man, "Where are you?" He answered, "I heard you in the garden, and I was afraid because I was naked; so, I hid."
Genesis 3:9-10

Self-worth is one of the areas where many people struggle. There are various reasons for this. From a trauma-filled childhood to painful words spoken over us or things we have done from a place of brokenness, we bear the label "unworthy" and allow it to define us. We carry it like a heavy weight on our shoulders, a burden.

Today's verse shows us that we can trace the damage to man's self-worth to the Garden of Eden, right at the fall, when Adam and Eve hid from God because they had sinned and suddenly felt ashamed to be in His presence. Their shame was built upon a lie though – that God didn't know what they had done. But God knew exactly what they had done, and that didn't stop Him from going to them as He always did. Instead, it stopped them from coming to Him. That bears repeating – God never stopped going to them; they stopped coming to Him.

God called. They hid.

That is what the enemy still tries to make us believe today: that we are disqualified from God's presence. He tells us we are sinners and, therefore, unworthy. He wants us to hide. The enemy knows the strength and freedom that come from choosing to be in the presence of God. To this day, he tries to cause us to hide.

God never stops coming to us, but we can stop going to him.

The devil uses our painful situations to lie to us. He uses our past, people, our setbacks or mistakes, or our appearance. We take one look at the mirror and recoil. Like Adam and Eve did, we want to hide because we are naked and don't like what we see. But remember this: the devil is a LIAR!

Our worth is not based on anything we think or feel. It cannot be determined by any human or demonic standard. Indeed, our worth cannot be increased nor reduced by anything that we do or did, or anything that was done or said to us. Our worth is not, nor will it ever be, based on our sins, appearance, behaviour or anything we can think or imagine.

Our worth is based on one simple truth – Jesus. It is determined by a God who thinks we are worthy and, therefore, sacrificed His life so we can keep ours. The truth is, our worthiness is not based on our performance but on our identity. It's not about what we do; it is about who we are - children of God. We are worthy because of our identity in Jesus.

If the saviour of the whole universe, the all-knowing, all-powerful, all-truthful God says we are wonderfully made, if

He says we are worthy and proves that by sacrificing His life for us, how dare we or anyone else think we are anything less than awesome? Are we calling God a liar?

God is not a man that He should lie! Nothing, absolutely nothing can or should separate us from the love of God.

Here are some scriptural truths that tell us who we are in Him:

- We are the apple of God's eye - Psalm 17:8
- We are God's delight - Zephaniah 3:17
- We are God's Masterpiece - Ephesians 2:10
- We are engraved in His hands - Isaiah 49:16
- We are adopted by God - Galatians 4:5
- We are shielded by His love - Psalm 5:12

We should never lie to ourselves or put ourselves down. We should never let anyone else define our worth any other way than through the eyes of Jesus and the freedom of the cross. Our God who took His time to create us considers us valuable and chose to send His son to die for us all. The cross was for you, me, and everyone (including the people you dislike or disagree with - yes, even them). We did not deserve it. We did not earn it.

Not only are we worthy, but we are also incredibly loved by God who accepts us as we are. His love is not dependent on our perfection; it is not even limited to the righteous. The Bible makes it clear in Romans 5:8: "But God demonstrates his own love for us in this: While we were still sinners, Christ died for us."

I know this to be true about God: He loves and accepts us exactly as we are. But in His great mercy and compassion, He does not leave us as we are. He is the healer of broken hearts. He is a redeemer and restorer. He is a way maker, the one who made a way for us to be in the right relationship with Him through His son. He is the same God who covered Adam and Eve by making clothes for them with His hands. That same gracious God considers us worthy. We are worthy!

BOLDer Statement

I am bold because I am worthy, fearfully and wonderfully made by God. I will step confidently into the presence of my God whose love never changes.

PRAYER

Dear Father,

I thank You for taking the time to create me perfectly for Your divine purpose. I thank You for placing within me everything I need to be the person You have called me to be. I pray You open my eyes to the truth of who I am in You, that as You take me on a journey of self-discovery, I find my true self that is hidden in Christ Jesus with God. In Jesus' name, Amen.

---

god's child

DAY 11

"Yet to all who did receive Him, to those who believed in His name, he gave the right to become children of God." John 1:12

"I am a child of God." This is such a profound statement filled with truth and promise, a statement so often said we can almost forget its significance. Well, maybe not you; maybe it's just me. I never knew I had adapted the saying so much it had become part of my Christian language, yet I probably never fully grasped how powerful and important the statement is.

I was listening to the book of John on my audio Bible when a familiar scripture took on a new meaning that has forever changed my perception of this statement.

I never fully understood the controversy about the statement, but the Jewish leaders certainly did. They knew what it meant and how powerful an association it was. The Bible tells us in John 5:17 that the Jewish leaders were furious and wanted to kill Jesus because he dared to say He was the son of

God. Their minds couldn't comprehend it (Also see John 10: 36-38).

It was a revolutionary statement at the time. It seemed ridiculous and impossible. It's like me walking about declaring I'm the daughter of the queen of England. Can I, a black commoner with no obvious royal connection, make such a bold claim? I would be sectioned or even arrested if I did. That was how outrageous it seemed at the time for Jesus to go about saying He was the son of God.

Hearing these scriptures quickened my spirit and humbled me. It reminded me how much of a privilege it is to have the freedom to call myself a child of God and to be a child of God. That is not just a statement but a fact. It is true. My self-esteem shot up, and I've been filled with godly confidence ever since.

Jesus paid the price on the cross. He died so we can have the liberty to embrace this identity. I'm challenged afresh to embrace my place as a daughter of the most high God, to walk in the fullness of my identity, knowing it is a precious gift, one that cost Jesus His life.

This immense revelation changed my perspective and deepened my relationship with Jesus. To think that more than 2,000 years ago, no one had the right or the privilege to be called children of God. Because of the cross, today, everyone who believes in Jesus Christ can embrace this identity and walk in its joy and fullness.

Your real identity has now been revealed:

- You are God's Child (Galatians 3:26).
- You are joint heirs with Jesus (Romans 8:17).

- God is your Father (2 Corinthians 6:18).
- You are no longer a slave but a child (Galatians 4:7).
- You are adopted into the family of God (Ephesians 1:5).

The Bible-based truths above should fill you with such joy and courage. Know who you are and whose you are. I encourage you to own it, embrace it and live it. Don't let the devil rob you of an identity that was bought with blood. It cost His life for you to be free to become a child of God, to have the freedom to approach God's throne with no barriers, no appointments or waiting lists.

This is the truth. This is your identity. This is who you are.

BOLDer Statement

I am bold because I am a child of God.

PRAYER

Dear Father,

Thank You for the privilege not just to be called a child of God but to be a child of God. I pray for the full manifestation of my identity in Christ Jesus. I pray that as I continue to grow in You, I walk boldly in the knowledge of my position in You and that I enjoy all the benefits of sonship. Today, I open my mouth to confess I am no longer a slave; I am a child of God. Thank You for all the prepared blessings You have in store for me. In Jesus' name, Amen.

---

a simple task

DAY 12

"Do not merely listen to the word, and so deceive yourselves. Do what it says." James 1:22

A few years ago, a lady from church asked to meet with me. She said God had put me on her heart to speak with urgently, so I met with her, humbled to serve in any way.

As she told me her story and how God had led her to me, I sat there confused, not knowing what to say or how to relate to experiences I'd never shared, so I did the only rational thing – I prayed with her.

I shared my story and some of my experiences and things that had helped me. I encouraged her to go for more prayer and attend some courses I knew would help. She was surprised at how simple it all sounded and I told her it's not by our might or power really but by God's grace.

We both left the meeting feeling certain all God wanted was for me to encourage her with His word and to pray with her, so I referred her to other ministries for more help and support. She promised to seek more help and left.

A few years later, I ran into her, and I was surprised to see she'd made little to no progress. She had not been to any of the places I referred her to and neither read the scriptures I shared nor done anything to help her situation since we met. At this time, she was sinking further into depression. We spoke briefly and she sounded bitter with herself and God. It saddened me, as I thought perhaps she expected much more out of the meeting with me was than I gave.

Sometimes God will direct us to people to get the help we need, but because we don't like the answer or we feel it's not good enough, too simple or maybe too expensive, we don't follow through. We obey partially by making contact but disobey by not using the information we get. We go from place to place asking for help, asking for advice and prayers, yet when we are told what to do, we don't follow through and then ask God why nothing has changed.

Who am I to judge? I'm guilty as well. There are times when I've done this same thing. I have asked for prayers and advice; I have been told what to do – REST. Just rest? Really? Is that all? It's so simple it makes no sense. I would not listen and would often suffer the consequence – being forced to rest by ill-health.

2 Kings 5 tells us the story of Naaman, a respected man who had leprosy. Elisha gave him a simple task – Go and wash in the river seven times and be healed. Annoyed by the sheer simplicity of the task, Naaman decided to walk away and almost missed his healing but for the intervention of a slave girl who reasoned with him. Perhaps he expected thunder and fire and spiritual fasting, prayers and all the works and

not just a dip in the river seven times. Eventually, his complete obedience gave him freedom from a despicable disease. It makes me wonder what our complete obedience will free us from if, as today's verse says, we do not merely listen to the word but do what it says. James was teaching about the importance of obedience and the blessing that comes with it.

Do you know it takes courage to obey? Being bolder means complete obedience. It means stepping out in faith and doing things that may seem foolish or easy. It means trusting God with all your heart and not leaning on your own understanding (Proverbs 3: 5-6).

What simple thing has God asked you to do? What instruction has He given you through someone? Have you completed the tasks and carried out the instructions? Could your disobedience be holding you captive?

I'd like to encourage you to try. Your freedom is at stake. Complete obedience will give you the life you're desperately praying for. God's instruction is not going to change. Just take courage and do what you've been told to do, no matter how simple, complicated or expensive it sounds.

Remember, His strength is made perfect in your weakness. If He asked you to do it, He would provide all the help and support you need. Just obey.

Here is a simple formula for dreams that come true:

Believe it with your heart.

Receive it with your mind.

Achieve it with your actions.

BOLDer Statement

I am bold because I have the faith and courage to obey God completely, regardless of how simple or complicated the task is.

PRAYER

Dear Father,

I pray for the courage to do all You ask me to do. I pray I do not interpret your instructions through the lens of my limited understanding but that now and always, I will trust in You and Your word. I ask You to reveal to me any area in my life where my disobedience has led to limitations and give me the strength I need to do what You say. I pray for the grace to not just be a hearer of the word but a doer of the word. In Jesus' name, Amen.

---

speak up for your blessing

DAY 13

"In her deep anguish, Hannah prayed to the Lord, weeping bitterly." 1 Samuel 1:10

Hannah was a woman in pain, sorrow and anguish, deeply saddened by the burden of childlessness in a home where she was being taunted by her husband's other wife. Her heart was broken and she was haunted by her helplessness, so she turned to God. Praying at the temple, she appeared drunk. When confronted by the priest, she was quick to explain her situation with humility and honesty, and she walked away with her blessing.

Today, many of us miss our blessings because we are too ashamed or too proud to share. We've stepped into a false life, the-fake-it-till-you-think-you've-made-it life and the "I'm fine" life. Instead of being honest with humility and sharing the truth of our burdens with people who can help, we keep quiet. Being bolder means being unafraid and unashamed to speak up and ask for help when we need it.

Like Hannah, be prepared to pour your heart out to the Lord. Pray for yourself. Do not just rely on the prayers of others. You must be willing to go to God and open your heart to Him. Eli met Hannah in a position of prayer, and it was her own words that he spoke a blessing over. He said, "Go in peace, and may the God of Israel grant you what you have asked of Him" (1 Samuel 1:17).

Are you praying? Don't just run from church to conference looking for someone to do for you what you have not started doing for yourself. As you can see from the verse above, Eli joined his faith with Hannah's and prayed over what she had already started to pray. Have you asked anything of God? You need to pray.

Be honest about your troubles with your pastor, prayer minister or whoever it is you can turn to for spiritual guidance. Don't pretend everything is okay. Share your burdens with boldness; you might walk away with answered prayers or with the help and support you need. But not all help is practical. Even if you need money, a prayer can open doors that are more profitable than cash.

Please don't run around looking for a "prophet" or a particular man or woman of God, assuming they can help you. God can use anybody; it is His power, not man's. Remember, God is the miracle worker, not man. Yes, some people are set apart by God and anointed to do great things, but God's power is not limited and cannot be contained. There is no formula with God. Do not put Him in a box. Unless the Holy Spirit leads you to seek out a particular person and you discern this correctly, do not limit God.

Your trust should be in God, not in any person, no matter how famous or popular they are. Like I said earlier, God can use anyone. That doesn't mean you should allow any random person to lay hands on you; please don't. Ask God for guidance. He will lead you to the right person, ministry or church.

Don't worry that people will laugh at you or judge you. Some may, but what's there to laugh at really? The truth is we ALL have issues. Every. Single. Person.

Even the bible says all have sinned. I'm not saying announce your trials on social media. Rather, I'm saying don't let fear and shame rob you of the chance to get the help you need. Plug into a good church, ministry or charity and ask for help. Be real when you need to. Let them pray for you and help you.

Be fearless in your pursuit of God's blessings. Don't allow shame, fear or insecurity to deprive you of a blessing that will change your life. Speak up. Speak out. Speak the truth. Prayer truly changes things.

BOLDer Statement

I am bold because I am not ashamed to speak up for my blessings. I will pour out my heart to God and the right person He has sent to help me.

PRAYER

Dear Father,

Thank You that I can come to you and share the burdens of my heart. I pray You bless me with the right people to pray over me, people You have appointed as vehicles for my answered prayer. I pray for wisdom and discernment to know who to go to and when. Teach me, Lord, to always place my trust in You and never put anyone in Your place. I confess all glory and honour will be Yours forever and ever. Amen.

good or god?

DAY 14

> "When the woman saw that the fruit of the tree was good for food and pleasing to the eye, and also desirable for gaining wisdom, she took some and ate it...." Genesis 3:6a

One morning, shortly after praying, God spoke quietly into my heart. Here's the summary of what He said: "When the woman saw that it was good, she ate, but that was not my will." The truth is, I was being reprimanded. For a few weeks, I had been dwelling on thoughts and making plans that in the eyes of the world would be good and acceptable but not in God's eyes.

As I pondered on Genesis 3:6, I knew immediately I was being reminded of a really important lesson: Just because something is good does not mean it is God. The devil was at work and he almost got me. Read carefully so he doesn't get you too.

The devil is not foolish. He would not deceive you with something bad. If he did, you'd see him coming from a mile off and run. If Eve had seen something bad or something that looked revolting, she wouldn't have eaten the fruit. The Bible tells us she saw it was good for food, pleasing, desirable – so she ate. Pause for a moment and reflect. Are you about to make a decision in your life right now based on what you can see? Just because it looks good, pleasing or desirable does not mean it is God's.

The portrayal of the devil as a scary beast has deceived us into thinking bad things are obvious and evil things are the real enemy. The truth is the enemy will come as a close friend or what appears like answered prayers. He mostly comes across as good, pleasing, and desirable; that is why he is called a deceiver. You will be looking at a lie.

The biggest distraction and deception the enemy uses to derail us from doing God's things is good things. Allow that to sink in. Meditate on it for a minute before you read on. Know this: the real enemy of the things of GOD is not bad things. That would be too easy. The enemy is not so foolish as to tempt you with obviously evil things. The real enemy of God's things is GOOD things. In fact, it can even be something godly. But if it is not the will of God for your life, then it is a hindrance, not a blessing.

This is why we need wisdom and discernment. This is why we need to test everything we do against God's will and word. This is why we need to be careful not to get carried away with the things that can distract us from our godly destiny. For example, God calls you to the mission field to serve Him and a few days before you go, you get an offer of a fantastic job with great perks. You start to think, "Wow, this is such a good thing. God has provided a way for me to earn a good living and fund someone else to go on the mission trip." Friends and family (like Adam) will agree to partake of that which looks good and encourage you to embrace this newfound blessing; some might even go so far as to say it is a miracle. Yet, it is the devil at work, preventing you from going on a mission that could lead to the freedom and salvation of many souls. Just like that, your gift as an evangelist has been buried by what is good but not of God.

I can share many examples from my personal life and the lives of others where the devil used good things to deceive God's children. If you take time to reflect, I am sure you will find some examples in your life. I hope today's message will be the wake-up call that empowers you to view life from a different perspective, one that sees you asking the question, "Is this good or God?" Not every gift is a blessing – some gifts will trap you into servitude. Not every promotion is a blessing – some promotions will leave you so busy, you won't even have time for God anymore. Not every open door is a blessing – even prisons have doors. I can go on, but I think you get the gist of what I am trying to teach you.

I will end with this truth: Every God thing is a good thing, but not every good thing is a God thing. Ask the Holy Spirit to help you discern. He is our helper.

Being bold means always choosing God over the apparent good. Sometimes that choice may come at the cost of being called foolish; choose God anyway.

BOLDer Statement

I am bold because I do not let good things distract me from God things.

PRAYER

Dear Jesus,

Thank you for Your word that brings revelation and wisdom. Open my eyes to see what is good but not of God and give me the grace and courage to change what I need to and let go of what is not of you. Protect me from the devices of the enemy, Lord, that I will continue to live in Your will and obey Your word for my life. In Jesus' name, Amen.

---

rejection or redirection?

DAY 15

"...But David found strength in the Lord his God." 1 Samuel 30:6b

Rejection can be extremely painful, especially when it is unexpected and undeserved. Many of us have been forsaken by the people we expect to love and accept us. But have you ever stopped to wonder if the rejection could be for your good? Come with me as I open the Word and show you that rejection can be redirection and that God is still in the midst of it all.

Let's look at 1 Samuel 29-30 and use King David as a case study. I encourage you to read these two chapters for yourself, but I'll give a quick summary.

David, while fleeing from Saul, settles with King Achish in the land of the Philistines. He and his army of 600 men, along with their wives and children, live in Ziklag in service to Achish. When the Philistines decide to go to war against Israel, Achish summons David and his men to join him in battle against Saul. However, the other Philistine kings reject

David (1 Sam 29:4-5). It pains Achish to tell David to go back home, and it hurts David to be rejected. He laments in verse 8, "What have I done to deserve this treatment?" King Achish reassures David, telling Him he had done nothing wrong, but he needs to return home the following morning.

Can you relate to this scenario? I certainly can. There have been times when I was rejected through no fault of mine. I had done everything right and had not deserved to be mistreated or misused, yet the rejection was swift and the hurt, relentless. It hurts. Many times, it comes from people close to you, people whom you expect will love and support you. Sometimes, people can reject you without meaning to. Like Achish, people can find themselves in a difficult situation where the choice is no longer theirs to make. That is a painful place to be.

Rejected and dejected, David journeys back home with his men, a journey that takes them three days. When they finally arrive, they find their town has been destroyed and their families and possessions gone. The Bible tells us in 1 Sam 30:3-4 that these men of war wept till they could weep no more and they were so bitter they even planned to stone David to death. I can only imagine what it would have felt like for these men to come back and see everything and everyone gone.

Then David strengthened himself in the Lord and enquired of God whether he should pursue them, and God said yes. They did so and recovered all that was lost and gained even more.

In those days, when kings went to war, the battle could last from weeks to months or, in some cases, years. So, take a minute and think about it. If David had not been rejected, if he had gone to war with his men, they would never have seen their families again.

What seemed like a painful rejection was, in reality, a redirection. It was God's divine intervention in the nick of time. Make no mistake, the kings were right to reject David; he was their enemy. They were going to war against the Israelites. David's disappointment was not out of loyalty to Achish. He wanted an opportunity to go to war and destroy God's enemies. He definitely would have switched sides if the opportunity presented itself. His intentions were good and maybe, in his disappointment, he may even have questioned God. God had a greater plan in mind, one that was merciful. Perhaps, it was more important to God that David and his men go back and recover all they lost than to go to war and kill God's enemies.

Which painful rejection are you still holding on to? Have you paused to reflect on the circumstances around the same time? If you do, you might see the hand of God at work. God always has a greater plan in mind. He truly works all things out for our good and His glory.

Know this truth today: Rejection can be redirection that leads to divine intervention.

Trust God in every situation you find yourself in and ask Him to open your eyes to see beauty in the ashes. Don't ever be afraid or ashamed to go back. You might just be in the nick of time to recover something or someone that would have been lost forever.

I know rejection is painful, and I am not saying it will be easy to understand or accept, but as David did, find strength in the

Lord your God. He has given us His Holy Spirit who is a gentle comforter to help us when we need Him.

BOLDer Statement

I am bold because I am not afraid to be rejected. I know God always has a great plan for my life.

PRAYER

Dear Father,

Thank You so much for the rejections You have used as redirections for me. I know You have good plans for my life, so I can rest in the knowledge that You are always at work even in the moments when I don't seem to understand what is happening. I pray for the grace to let go of the offences that have arisen from the rejections in my life. Help me to forgive all those who have hurt me and to release them into Your loving arms. In Jesus' name. Amen.

---

grateful always

DAY 16

"Give thanks in all circumstances; for this is God's will for you in Christ Jesus." 1 Thessalonians 5:18

I remember clearly when I first heard this scripture spoken aloud. I was barely twelve years old. My mother had come into the house screaming at the top of her voice, "In all circumstances give thanks to God" or something very close to that. A few hours before, my older brother had been taken to the hospital with a sickle cell crisis, so when I heard my mother crying and praising God, I got excited, thinking a miracle had happened. What I didn't know was that my brother had just died. I was furious. How dare she thank God for that?

For many years, that image has sat with me, and it has encouraged and discouraged me in equal measure. I didn't understand it initially, but over the years as I've matured in my relationship with God, I have realised that my mum wasn't giving thanks because she was happy. Instead, she was crying out from the depths of her soul to the God she loved, declaring her trust in Him to see her through the death of her only son. She was turning away from her pain and facing God with His word. That moment taught me one of the most significant spiritual lessons I have ever learnt. My mother laid a foundation that did not tell me to trust God. She showed me to trust God.

As the world continues to come to terms with the effects of the COVID pandemic, the cost-of-living crisis, the high interest rates, numerous earthquakes, the ongoing war in Ukraine, the shootings in America and our everyday challenges, today's verse can seem so out of place and difficult for many. You may read this verse and ask, "What is there to give thanks for or how can I give thanks when my life is falling apart?" It makes no sense.

As I read and meditated on this scripture, God laid a few things on my heart to share. I have done this by breaking down the words in the verse.

"Give thanks in all circumstances" - No matter the circumstance, whether good or bad, God asks us to give thanks. I think it is important to note He doesn't ask us to **feel** thankful but to **be** thankful. Our ability to give thanks to God should not depend on how we feel; it should depend on our willingness to obey God's word. God knows what He is asking us to do may be difficult, but it truly is for our good. When we choose to give thanks, we change our focus from ourselves (powerless to change the situation) to a God who is all-powerful and able to change the situation we face and bring us peace and comfort.

Sometimes, we like a good moan. It can feel much easier to focus on our problems, talk about them, think about them, cry about them and be overwhelmed by them. Yet, we can't do anything by ourselves to change them. But God can. This verse is not telling us to be thankful for things that have caused us pain; it is saying we should be thankful despite the things that have caused us pain because we know we serve a God who is trustworthy and is in control of everything. Prov. 3:5 asks us to trust in the Lord with all our hearts and not lean on our own understanding. We may never understand our trials in life, but we don't need to if we truly lean on, depend on and trust in God.

There is always something to be thankful for. Find it and give thanks to God. Put emotions aside and you'll find God's grace still at work. Even amid painful circumstances, God is still doing great things, and our ability to give Him thanks is the foundation for His ability to turn beauty into ashes. When Jesus found Himself in difficult circumstances such as having to feed the 5,000 or at the last supper before He was betrayed, the Bible records He broke bread and gave thanks. Out of His thanksgiving, multiplication and miracles happened.

"God's will for you in Christ Jesus" - Simply put, this is what God wants us to do in Jesus' name. As children of God, we are called to obey. God loves an obedient heart; it is a heart that trusts Him completely and puts hope in Him. Our willingness to do God's will is important and, to be honest, not always easy. This is why we must do it in Christ Jesus. We don't have to do it alone; we can ask for help. In fact, we should ask for help. We can call on Jesus to help us give thanks. The Bible says He lives forever to intercede on our behalf (Hebrews 7:25). He is our high priest. In Him, we can find the strength we need to give thanks even when our hearts and minds are burdened by painful circumstances and we don't feel thankful.

We do not serve a God who doesn't understand pain and suffering. We do not serve a God who is asking us to do something He never had to do. I can't imagine what it must have been like for Jesus, sitting with His disciples, one of whom He knew would betray Him, at the Last Supper breaking bread and giving thanks. Jesus knew He would be crucified, yet He still gave thanks.

There is always something to be thankful for in every situation. Find it, hold on to it as that is hope in your hands. Give it to God in prayer and keep searching for things to be thankful for every day. Write them down so you don't forget, and when fear and anxiety kick in, you can go back to read them and praise God.

BOLDer Statement

I am bold because I give thanks regardless of how I feel.

PRAYER

Dear Lord,

I pray for the grace to give thanks always, especially in those moments when I feel anxious and overwhelmed. Teach me to focus on You and not on my circumstances that I have no power to change. I pray for a tender heart that trusts completely in You, and according to Your will, I will always give you thanks every day of my life. In Jesus' name. Amen.

rest to recharge

DAY 17

"Truly my soul finds rest in God; my salvation comes from him." Psalm 62:1

In the busyness of the world, we may find it difficult to rest. I had a funny experience a few years ago that reminded me how important it is to rest. One morning, while I was getting ready for work, I picked up my electric toothbrush and turned it on. Nothing happened. There was no buzz. I had forgotten to rest it on the charger to charge it. It was dead and powerless. I was already running late and had no time to charge and use it, so I had no choice but to use the electric toothbrush like a manual toothbrush. It was useful but not effective. It was not designed to be used in that way. With every stroke of the soft, lifeless bristles on my teeth, I was annoyed with myself, and I knew that my mouth was not as clean as it should be. I remember hiding away the best part of that day, refusing to engage in conversations that would put me in proximity with anyone.

That experience taught me the importance of resting to recharge. It taught me that if we do not intentionally rest in Jesus, we will be dull and lifeless – useful but not powerful enough to be effective in all God has called us to do.

I've learned that when we rest in God, it is His time to recharge us. The purpose of rest is to get energy, and we need spiritual energy too. We rest to recharge. If we do not rest, we will not have the boldness and confidence that come from being charged up spiritually.

We may shy away from our gifts and callings without knowing it. Perhaps, we walk in fear and uncertainty, avoiding anything that requires faith. Just like I avoided getting close to others that fateful day.

Being bold means we are proactive in truly finding rest in God, that we take the time to plug in and do nothing whilst His Spirit breathes life into us as we soak into His word. Then, we will be strengthened and renewed.

"Remain in me, as I also remain in you. No branch can bear fruit by itself; it must remain in the vine. Neither can you bear fruit unless you remain in me" (John 15:4). We cannot successfully be who God has called us to be without taking the time to rest in the true vine and abide in Him.

There are two types of rest that we need to recharge:

1. Physical Rest – This is so important. God wants us to rest. He declared the Sabbath as a commandment and not a suggestion because He knows the importance of rest for the human body he created. Much of the sickness and disease we face today comes as a result of the disobedience to the Sabbath. Our bodies were not created to be under the stress of work seven days a week. The devil likes us to be busy, so if we

let him, he will create opportunities for us to weary ourselves with good things that are unnecessary. A tired Christian is easy prey for the devil. Be wary of being too busy to rest your body; make it a priority to observe the sabbath rest.

2. Spiritual Rest – This is also an important rest, where we deliberately unplug from the things of this world so we can focus on our spiritual growth. One of the ways we can rest is through fasting, where we take time to let go of food and feast on God's Word. When you fast, prioritise the word, prayers and worship and draw strength from intimacy with God. The Bible tells us "But they that wait upon the LORD shall renew their strength; they shall mount up with wings as eagles; they shall run, and not be weary; and they shall walk, and not faint" (Isaiah 40:31 KJV).

Just like physical rest, we need to discipline our bodies to fast regularly. I try to fast one day a week as a habit, but I also have moments of extended fasts as led by the Holy Spirit.

Out of our resting comes the strength we need to be the warriors God has called us to be. Rest to recharge!

BOLDer Statement

I am bold because I make rest a priority in my life.

PRAYER

Dear Father,

Teach me how to rest fully in You. Open my eyes to see the deception of the enemy, causing me to always be busy with no room for rest. Give me the grace to be more organised and to make rest a priority. I pray for the strength and discipline to fast, study and worship, that I may abide in You and always be connected to the true vine. In Jesus name, Amen.

---

alone is too much

DAY 18

"You and these people who come to you will only wear yourselves out. The work is too heavy for you; you cannot handle it alone." Exodus 18:18

Exodus 18 verse 13 onwards, tells an interesting story about the need for community in leadership. This story is set during the exodus of God's people from Egypt to the promised land. Jethro watches his son-in-law Moses spend countless hours being a judge for the people. It is cumbersome and tiring. He then calls him aside and teaches him a simple method for effective management, which can be summarised in two key points:

1. Equip the people to learn self-management - "Teach them his decrees and instructions, and show them the way they are to live and how they are to behave" (v20).
2. Delegate authority - "Train up other leaders, select capable men and set them over thousands, hundreds, fifties, and tens" (v 21).

We can learn a lot from this story, and I encourage you to read Exodus 18:13-27 carefully and allow God to teach you through His word a more effective way to manage your time and the people He has called you to serve. Also, we must learn that we are not called to do life alone. We need others' help to be effective in doing that which God has called us to do.

When the weight of responsibility knocks on your door this week, don't try to do everything yourself. It is not just dangerous for you; it is also dangerous for those you are called to serve – "You and these people who come to you will only wear yourselves out. The work is too heavy for you; you cannot handle it alone" (Ex 18:18).

Today's verse is one of the verses that hits you right in the gut and needs little explanation. The Bible is clear: we cannot do it alone, whatever IT might be. But that does not stop us from trying, does it? The simple truth is we need the help of others, and when we share the responsibility, it not only makes the load lighter but frees us up to handle the weightier matters. Stop trying to do it all on your own. It is not a sign of good leadership or godly wisdom. Moses received wise counsel from His father-in-law and put in place a strategy that brought peace to him and the Israelites.

Acts 6:1-4 also teaches us the importance of delegating responsibility. When the apostles were faced with the troubling matter of food distribution, they knew they could not do everything themselves, so they chose to focus on the ministry of the Word and had seven others wait on tables.

God will show you the areas in your life where you are trying to do things alone, leaving you tired and burnt out. Being bolder means identifying the things YOU must do by yourself and knowing the things that you can get support for.

BOLDer Statement

I am bold because I will not try to do things alone. I receive help from others.

PRAYER

Dear Father,

Thank You for teaching me the importance of sharing my life with others. I pray You bless me with the right people to support and empower me to be all You have called me to be. I pray for wisdom and discernment to recognise my destiny helpers and to honour them. I pray You show me ways I can help others so that because of my presence, they can fulfil their God-given assignment. In Jesus' name, Amen.

---

the heart of a centurion

DAY 19

> "The centurion replied, "Lord, I do not deserve to have you come under my roof. But just say the word, and my servant will be healed" Matthew 8:8

Matthew 8: 5-13 tells the story of a Roman Centurion whose faith in Jesus was so strong it earned him a spot in this great book. Whilst the emphasis of this story is often the *faith* of the centurion, I am also intrigued about the *heart* of the centurion.

This man came to Jesus in Capernaum, asking for help. He had a servant lying paralysed and sick in his household. The centurion pleaded with Jesus not for his wife or his child but for a servant. He came all the way looking for Jesus to heal HIS SERVANT! What was it about the servant that made this well-respected man seek out Jesus?

A Roman Centurion many years ago was a man to be respected. As his name implies, he was in charge of at least a century (100 soldiers). In some cases, a centurion may take charge of 60 centuries which became a legion. The Bible did not specify which centurion this man was, but what we do know is he was by no means an ordinary man. He could have sent any of the 100 soldiers in his command. He could even have sent another servant, but instead, he came himself, seeking healing from Jesus for his servant.

Take a minute to think about that. Three things stand out to me:

- The faith and respect he had in and for Jesus
- The love and sense of responsibility he had for his servant
- The faith he had in Jesus even though neither he nor his servant were Jews

I'm not sure why this story always makes me emotional. It certainly makes me stop and ask – is this common practice today? Are there people willing to intercede on behalf of others? Are there leaders who will fight for the lives of those who look up to them? Who will you take to Jesus? Being bolder means thinking of the needs of others, not just our family or friends but also the people God places in our lives, regardless of who they are and what they do. We show love by having the courage to take people to Jesus.

Today's verse should not only show us the importance of faith, but also lead us to question the position of our hearts. There are questions we must ask ourselves:

- How good are we at providing the people who support, serve, or report to us in any capacity with opportunities for growth?
- How good are we at loving others to the extent that their burdens become ours and we are willing to step

out in faith and take their needs to Jesus in prayer personally?

The Bible was clear. The Centurion understood authority, and he had an army at his command. He could have sent anyone. Yet, he went himself to Jesus whom the religious leaders of the time were rejecting. The centurion was not even a Jew. He was a Roman soldier. Yet, this unnamed centurion had a heart filled with love that compelled him to action and a faith that was so strong even Jesus was baffled.

BOLDer Statement

I am bold because I have a heart that loves others so much. I am willing to intercede for them.

PRAYER

Dear Father,

I pray not just for the faith of the centurion but that You bless me with the heart of the centurion. I pray for a heart that is willing to be an intercessor and speak up for those who are paralysed in various life situations. I pray for a heart that is willing to go to Jesus in faith for those whom others may consider undeserving. I pray for a loving heart that compels me to action. In Jesus' name. Amen.

---

freedom in christ

DAY 20

> "It is for freedom that Christ has set us free. Stand firm, then, and do not let yourselves be burdened again by a yoke of slavery." Galatians 5:1

When Paul wrote today's verse, he wanted to remind the converted Christians that Jesus died to set them free. Jewish leaders were teaching the Galatians to return to the law of Moses, telling them they needed to be circumcised and to follow other laws to be truly saved. But if the law was able to bring salvation, then Jesus died for nothing.

Have you ever felt imprisoned? I have heard stories of Christians being put under a yoke of slavery by ministers of faith who misinterpret God's Word to suit their selfish desires. There is a lot of church hurt and, sadly, cases of abuse where God's children are walking around with burdens and yokes too painful to carry. This is not what Jesus died for us to have; this is not what the cross was for.

Paul encouraged the Gentiles to stand firm in their freedom and not let themselves be burdened again by yokes of slavery. Today, be encouraged as well to stand firm. Know God's Word for yourself. Being bolder means you know the truth of who you are in Christ Jesus and do not allow yourself to be manipulated and controlled in a way that is contrary to God's will. Although the context today may be different, the principles are still the same. We are free in Christ Jesus: that's a truth we can hold on to.

Here are three important things I learned as I meditated on this scripture:

1. Jesus died so we can be free, not only in our bodies but also in our minds. The yoke of slavery is not usually physical; it is most often spiritual. Sometimes, people will try to put us in mental bondage, playing with our thoughts and emotions, and using words and behaviours that can leave us feeling like captives. That is not God's will.
2. It is our responsibility to stand firm. The world has plenty of fear and anxiety to throw at us, but we cannot let ourselves be burdened or entangled or submit again to yoke of slavery. The word 'again' is critical. It means we've been delivered of this before, so we must choose not to be enslaved to sin again. Slavery is a mindset. Our lives are not in the hands of the world; our lives are in God's hands.
3. We can listen to advice from the world, and we can embrace the laws that society dictates are necessary, but ultimately, we must take our direction from the truth of God's Word, which says Christ died so we can be free.

Rest in this truth. Meditate on this word, and allow God to minister to you. Let it bring you comfort, assurance and true freedom, a freedom in Christ that empowers you to be all God has called you to be.

BOLDer Statement

I am bold because I have freedom in Christ Jesus.

PRAYER

Dear Lord,

Thank You for setting me free. Help me to live in the fullness of the freedom You died for me to have and deliver me from anything or anyone that seeks to hold me captive again. I pray for the grace I need to not imprison myself with my thoughts, words or actions, but instead, live my life knowing I am free to be the woman You have called me to be. In Jesus' name, Amen.

---

the throne of god

DAY 21

"Let us then approach God's throne of grace with confidence, so we may receive mercy and find grace to help us in our time of need." Hebrews 4:16

On the 27th of March 2020, I found myself in a familiar place called despair. Watching the news left me feeling overwhelmed. It was all about covid, death and chaos. It didn't help that I also felt unwell. My conversations with myself were filled with discouragement, disappointment, faith, hope and fear in equal amounts. How could I be so weak? Shouldn't I know better seeing that even in despair I still had my mustard seed faith?

As I knelt to pray, I felt unqualified to take communion and pray. The enemy was quick to remind me of my flaws and weaknesses, but I prayed anyway because I knew God had called me to intercede and pray. I was doing a fourteen-day prayer and communion session as led by the Holy Spirit, but on that particular day, I just felt so discouraged.

That morning, God guided me to today's verse. I was reminded that Jesus understands my weaknesses and flaws, and they do not in any way disqualify me or anyone else from coming to God in prayer. The Bible says in Hebrews 4:15 that Jesus understands and can empathise with us. He truly knows what it's like to be human.

Perhaps, like I was, you're struggling to keep your faith and hope alive. Perhaps you are asking God some hard questions, and you feel overwhelmed and afraid – you find yourself unable to pray, unable to praise and you feel distant from God.

I don't know about you, but my life is an exercise of grace. I need it. I'm an imperfect child of God with many flaws. Only His daily grace holds me together. It gives me the courage to be honest and not pretend I am holier than anyone else. It's normal to be worried and anxious, to question God and to wonder about these uncertain times. We are human with flaws, after all. But let these emotions be an event (something that happens), not a destination (a place you go to and stay). Don't dwell in despair.

Being bolder means you know you can always go to God. It doesn't matter who you are, what you have done or how you feel. The Father always has His hands open, waiting to receive you. The devil will lie to you and remind you of your mistakes. He will try to trick you into thinking you are disqualified from or unqualified to be in God's presence. Do not fall for the devil's tricks or believe his lies. Nothing can ever separate you from the love of God.

Today's scripture is an invitation from God to us all. He wants us to come boldly to His throne, where we will find everything we need. When all those overwhelming emotions come, the throne is the place to go not the place to run from. God is calling us to Him. We all need God's mercy and grace in the various seasons of life. His mercy will deliver and save us all and His grace will protect, guide, comfort and heal us. Boldly approach His throne today. He is waiting for you.

BOLDer Statement

I am bold because I know I can go to His throne for mercy and help.

PRAYER

Dear Father,

I thank You, for You are always willing to receive me, and Your grace and mercy are sufficient for me. Help me to come to You with confidence, knowing that in You is everything I need to live fully. Teach me to not rely on how I feel but on the truth of Your word. In Jesus' name. Amen.

---

let go and forgive

DAY 22

"Be kind and compassionate to one another, forgiving each other, just as in Christ God forgave you."
Ephesians 4:32

Life is full of them, isn't it? Annoying people and situations, disappointments, discouragements, and dashed hopes. There is wickedness and injustice. No wonder it's so easy for us to be offended and justifiably. It makes sense to be annoyed, especially when it's not your fault. But the truth is, we need to let go of the hurt and move on. God wants us to forgive one another.

Matthew 18: 23-35 tells us the parable of the unforgiving servant. It is one of my favourite stories in the Bible. In this parable, a king chooses to forgive a servant's debt worth millions, but that same servant refuses to forgive a debt of hundreds. When the king finds out, he punishes the unforgiving servant and holds him in bondage until he pays off his debt. When you read this parable, you may be quick to say what a wicked servant he is, but the truth is, there is an unforgiving servant in each of us. When we choose to hold on to offence and not forgive others, we are no different from the servant in that parable.

God has forgiven us so much and we will never know how much it truly cost God to reconcile us with Him through His son, Jesus. We are quick to forget we are sinners forgiven daily by a God who loves us. Why then can't we forgive others?

Unforgiveness is like a poison that robs you of so much. It sits in you and sucks the life out of you. It's like holding yourself captive with bitterness and anger while trying to live a normal life but making no progress.

Offences are shackles that weigh you down. You can never walk in freedom with an offended heart. When you hold on to offence, you imprison yourself and pollute your heart with negativity. You grieve the Holy Spirit by creating an inhospitable environment. When your spirit is grieved, your physical body bears the burden of your mental decision to hold grudges.

Sometimes, the person you need to forgive most is yourself. I know this to be true in my own life. I used to be so hard on myself, angry with myself for the mistakes I made, for the things I should have done but didn't do. God showed me that offence is a self-imposed prison because as much as I was upset with myself, I could not make the right changes. I started to see myself flourish and grow only when I allowed God to work in me and give me the grace to let go of my disappointments.

Sometimes, the devil will cause offence to fester in our hearts, not only against ourselves or other people in our lives but also against situations and circumstances beyond our control. We can get offended by climate change, religious leaders, economic disasters, organisations, political leaders, countries, nations etc. These types of offences can limit us and leave us bitter and angry with the world, with God, and with life. The devil places offence in our hearts to steal our peace. That is not the will of God for our lives. Jesus was punished for our peace (Isaiah 53:5). He died and left His peace with us (John 14:27). Don't give the devil the right to cause you to live with an offence that steals your peace that came at a huge cost. Let go of offence and protect your peace.

There are so many other stories in the Bible that teach us the importance of forgiveness. God's stance is clear: if we don't forgive others, we will not be forgiven ourselves (Matthew 6:15). Holding on to an offence is walking in direct disobedience to God's Word. God says we should forgive. You cannot say you love God and live a life with offence because obedience is the manifestation of love. If you love God, you will obey His word (John 14:15).

Choosing not to remain offended is not pretending that you were not wronged., It's not justifying the situation either. Instead, you are saying, "God, I trust You, and because I love You, I will obey Your word regardless of my feelings. I put Your word first." True strength lies in your ability to allow God to be the judge and to love the unlovable.

You need to free yourself from yourself for yourself. Forgiveness is for you; it sets you free. Choose to not remain offended. Ask God to help you. It's not easy, especially when the offence is huge and cuts deep, but it's worth it. A wise man once said, "Being offended is an event, remaining offended is a decision." It is your choice. You get to choose – will you let God be the judge or do you want to help him?

Sit for a minute and check your heart; are you offended? Is there anything or anyone you need to bring to Jesus' feet? He is waiting with His arms wide open.

BOLDer Statement

I am bold because I forgive and let go.

PRAYER

Dear Father,

I am thankful for Your word and Your grace and mercy over my life. I ask You to help me forgive and let go; I cannot do it by myself, but with your help, I know I can do anything. I ask You to remind me of every person I have not forgiven and give me the grace to let go. Please, show me the people I have offended and give me the courage to make things right. In Jesus' name, Amen.

---

be a blessing

DAY 23

"Then Peter said, "Silver or gold I do not have, but what I do have I give you. In the name of Jesus Christ of Nazareth, walk." Acts 3:3

Today, God will give you an opportunity to bless someone. Take it. Blessing someone does not always mean spending money. The Bible shows us that some of the greatest blessings did not cost anything.

Today's verse is from Acts 3:2-10, which tells the story of a lame man at the gate called Beautiful. He had been lame from birth, which was very hard in those times. He begged for alms at the gate every day, hoping to get some money to survive. While Peter and John were passing by, he asked them for money, but they gave him something better. They healed him in the name of Jesus.

Peter had no money, but he gave the man what he had, and it was exactly what the man needed. The man walked for the first time in his life. He was so happy that he jumped and praised God. What a wonderful sight at the gate called Beautiful. Can you imagine? Maybe God wants to use you to make someone's life beautiful too.

Blessing someone is not about what you lack; it's about what you have and are willing to share. It may be small or seemingly insignificant, but it may just be exactly what someone needs today. I have seen God do big things with little things. He can multiply your gift and make it a miracle in someone's life. What are you willing to give up to bless someone? A little boy gave up his lunch, and God used it to feed 5,000 men. He gave his little, and God made it much more.

Today, I encourage you to bless someone. Be bold and do something kind for someone. Give a hug, a smile, a word of encouragement, practical help or like Peter, pray. Don't ever underestimate the power of prayer. It is powerful, free, and the best gift you can give anyone. It is love in action.

Being bolder means you are intentional about blessing others. You are willing to do what you can, when you can. You don't have to be rich to make a difference in someone's life; you just have to care enough to try. Love has no price tag.

Prayer works and it's not about your ability, but God's. You can't change anything by yourself, but God can, and He loves to. So don't be afraid. Step out boldly and pray for someone today. You never know who will rejoice and praise God because of your prayer.

BOLDer Statement

I am bold because I care about the people in my world and take proactive steps to be a blessing.

PRAYER

Dear Lord,

Give me the opportunity to bless someone today. Fill my heart with love and compassion for your people so I can show my love for You through my love for others. I pray that through me, you will answer prayers that fill someone with joy and praise for you. Use me, Lord, to bring a testimony into the lives of others. In Jesus' name. Amen.

PS: Some scriptures come with conditions that require us to act. Don't quote them blindly. If there is an action attached to the promise, then do it. Working the Word is a partnership; do your part and God will do His.

Storms of life!

DAY 24

Storms can be destructive, breaking windows, blowing down trees and causing traffic conditions that lead to chaos and endanger lives. Thunder and lightning rip through the skies with a mixture of deafening sounds and blinding lights, leaving trembling infants clinging to anything or anyone for comfort. Storms can be cruel, loud, wet, windy and dark.

Sometimes, the trials we face in life leave us feeling like we are right in the midst of a raging storm. We are deafened by the noise and blinded by the light. We are wet to our bones from the downpour of rain and shivering with clenched teeth. When a storm comes, it can be small, big or never-ending torrential rain, leaving us confused and in despair. It can overwhelm us and take our breath away.

Sometimes, we ask in whispers but most often out loud, "Where is God?" We may even ask, "Is Jesus asleep in the boat?" Amidst painful tears that feel like they are birthed from heavy, grey clouds, we lie awake at night, tossing and turning, plagued by unshakable anxiety and pondering one simple question: "WHY"?

It's like a quiet drum and a loud piano playing a soulful tune with lyrics of woe and choruses of self-pit. As we turn to our inner strength and rely on our wisdom and fail woefully, we are gripped by fear. The storm is fierce, loud, and terrifying, with no sign of surrender or retreat. Is this your story today? Read on; there is hope.

This storm. What does it seek? Is there anything left to give? Why is it here? Will life ever be the same again? Can you withstand the storm? Questions ripple through your aching soul, unanswered, unspoken, unheard. The loneliness is crushing, making a soft but audible noise, like the sound of heavy feet crushing dried autumn leaves.

In a busy world, the storms of life can make you feel isolated as though you are the only one who can hear, see, and feel them. It's as if they were designed for you. Yet, most storms are visible to all, leaving you ashamed as you think everyone knows. Worse still, the impact is not just on you; it affects those you love, those who look up to you and those waiting to mock you.

Then, just as you start to dwell on your circumstances, you hear a small but firm voice that urges and invites you with intimate words: "Look at Me, beloved, and fear not." The words, barely above a whisper, can be easily missed as they are not always audible. Sometimes they are hidden in the pages of His word that you have forgotten to open for weeks.

Therein lies your relief from the storms of life: Being rooted in the Lord of the storm and resting firmly on the One who sleeps in a storm because He has the power to rebuke it. Don't receive the spirit of fear or self-pity; don't look at the waves and lose focus. The Bible tells us what to do: "Instead, put on the Lord Jesus Christ, and make no provision for the flesh, to gratify its desires." Romans 13:14 NRSV

PUT ON JESUS! Wear Him around you. Don't give in to the flesh that wants to scream fear and defeat. Make no provision for it. Again, I say: Put on the Lord Jesus Christ. The power to overcome storms is not in the possession of the Word but in its application. Put Jesus on! Let Him be your covering.

This is what happens when you do: The mist and fog lift and you are confronted with the miraculous truth as it unveils itself before you. The storm that is meant to cause damage and destruction is the same storm God has used to clear your path. Wow! It is not destruction but redirection. Won't God bring beauty from ashes? Isn't that His word? Does He lie?

See how God uses storms.

Storms open closed doors, make the impossible possible, and wash away hindrances. They awaken the dreams that fear had shut down and create a clear path towards healing, restoration, and self-discovery. They lead us to God's secret place and His light, where we experience deeper intimacy with Him, born out of sorrow, anxiety, and grief. Storms can produce trust, hope, faith, and courage. The storm may cause pain, but it also fulfils purpose. Pain does not mean defeat or failure

The truth is simple: God can use the same storm that was meant to destroy you to restore you. You may feel displaced, but you will be repositioned for greatness.

My prayer for you today, and always, is that you don't give up, especially in the middle of a raging storm. I urge you to keep hoping, trusting, and holding on to Jesus, even if you only have the strength to touch the hem of His garment.

Remember this: our saviour truly saves, and the storms of life are no match for the one who commands the wind and the seas and they obey Him.

the art of praying scripture

DAY 25

Praying Scripture is the art of speaking God's truth over and into your life. God acts according to His Word. He only does what He has promised in His word.

As a child of God, you have the right to say, "Father, You said (insert the scripture for the situation)" when you pray. The Bible teaches us that God's Word never returns void (Isaiah 55:11); it accomplishes what He intends. So, if God has spoken, then pray that Word until you see it manifested in your life. You have the right to stand on His word. That is the kind of prayer that moves God's hand and heart.

We often pray amiss (John 4:3). Our motives are questionable when we rely on our own thinking, and then we wonder why God is silent or why our prayers are not answered. It is not because God is powerless or unable to answer but because we don't ask according to His will for our lives, or we don't ask Him to do what He has said. Silence is often the result, which can frustrate us. But I have good news: praying scripture effectively can bring the change and transformation you seek. God wants to hear you speak His Word because He wants to answer you with His Word. He is faithful to His Word. He is not a man; He does not lie (Numbers 23:19).

Take the time to study His word and find out what He has said about your situation. Sometimes, we think we are going to God in prayer when we are only grumbling and complaining. We speak words that do not edify us; we give power to negative situations by repeating lies and pains instead of speaking truth and life. We go to God with just our problems, moaning and complaining, when the Bible shows how much God hates complaining. It is a useless waste of time.

I am not saying we cannot take our burdens to God. After all, He said we can cast them all to Him because He cares (1 Peter 5:7). But let that not be the only thing you take to God. When you go to God, back it up with His word and remind Him what He said. "It is written" is such a powerful phrase. It is a weapon you can and should use to disarm the devil. You need to speak what is written concerning you and everyone else.

Praying scripture builds up faith, encourages you, affirms you, and helps you pray according to God's will. If you find yourself in a place where you are discouraged and depressed, get into His Word. Personalise it and speak it out. Faith comes by hearing the Word of God.

Here is an example of how I pray scripture. I will use Genesis 26:13 (NKJV): "The man began to prosper, and continued to prosper until he became very prosperous."

I personalise it by praying my name and claiming prosperity by faith. I pray, "Amanda began to prosper and continued prospering until she became very prosperous." I speak this over my life with strong conviction knowing God's Word is true and Jesus came as a revelation and fulfilment of every promise. Hallelujah!

Today, I am indeed prosperous in Jesus' name according to His Word, not just financially, but also in my soul, my family, my health, and my ministry. Everything that concerns me prospers. I believe what God says He can and will do. I truly believe in the Word of God. As I pray and rehearse this scripture, my mind is renewed, and my spirit is opened up to new ideas that make the manifestation of this word possible. It is not that this word works like magic. No, it doesn't. God is not a magician; He is a miracle worker, which means He does the impossible, but we need to do what is possible in His name.

The Bible teaches us it is God who gives power to get wealth (Deuteronomy 8:18). He is also the one who teaches us to profit (Isaiah 48:17). So, whenever He brings good ideas, I put in the work to follow them through. For example, it is 1.31 am, and I am here typing instead of sleeping. God gives me the wisdom to write and the grace to execute, and then He blesses the project in a way that brings prosperity. I have prospered, and I continue to enjoy the prosperity of God in all areas of my life. As someone who was sick and broke for many years, I can say that today I am the healthiest version of myself and more financially secure than I have ever been because I believed, prayed with faith, read His Word, and put my faith into action.

Why not put your name in this scripture and pray it fervently, claiming the truth of His Word? The Bible says we should put God in remembrance of His word (Isaiah 43:26), not because He has forgotten, but because we have remembered. Pray His

Word with confidence. This is one of the most powerful things you can do. It is the most effective way to pray.

Over the next six days. I will show you how to 'pray scripture' using some Bible verses that have blessed me tremendously and that I speak over my life. I hope it encourages you to pray the Word.

praying scripture - 1

DAY 26

"I keep asking that the God of our Lord Jesus Christ, the glorious Father, may give me the Spirit of wisdom and revelation, so that I may know him better." Ephesians 1:17 (personalised)

In this scripture, I'm praying the words of Apostle Paul over my life. I have personalised it to make it mine, asking God by faith. Take a minute and read the scripture out loud and then read it again. Wow, isn't it powerful?

Have you been praying for wisdom? Do you crave a revelational knowledge of Jesus? Have you been praying for intimacy with Him but still feel so far away? It is time to pray scripture and put God in remembrance of His word.

Today's verse, spoken with humility and sincerity, has the power to change your life. You are asking God for the Spirit of wisdom and revelation. Why? So, you may know Him better. Pray this scripture with faith, and you will receive. God wants you to know Him.

"Father, you said." – this is your right as a child. You are speaking to your Father who cannot lie. If He said it, He will do it. And if you say it with faith and in the correct context, He will hear and answer. You will be transformed.

Don't go to God empty-handed. Go with His word. The Bible is full of great things God has said. Remind Him what He said concerning you, not because He has forgotten, but because you have remembered.

If you don't know the truth of His word, the devil will feed you with lies. Satan will tell you that you are weak, sick, broke, unworthy, etc. All these are lies.

The Bible says:

- You are strong - Joshua 1:9
- You are healed - Isaiah 53:5
- You are rich - James 1:9
- You are worthy - Psalm 139:14

Knowledge of the word is powerful, necessary, and liberating. Pray the Word of God into reality in your life. Rev. Kenneth Hagin said, "Confession comes before possession." Don't let the enemy rob you of the fullness of life Jesus died for you to have. Be committed to confessing and possessing from today.

PS: Some scriptures come with conditions that require us to act. Don't quote them blindly. If there's an action attached to the promise, then do it. Working the Word is a partnership; do your part and God will do His.

praying scripture - 2

DAY 27

> "I am joyful in hope, patient in affliction, faithful in prayer." Romans 12:12

Words are incredibly powerful. The Bible teaches us that God spoke this world into existence. He created it with His words and made it with His hands. Since we are made in His image and likeness, we must understand that the words we speak have the power to create, which is why we must be mindful of our speech.

The world has caught on to the power of words. You hear things like positive declarations or daily affirmations etc. These are good things. But instead of just saying any word because it sounds nice, declare words from THE WORD. This is another way to effectively pray scripture. Don't just do the good thing, do the God thing. Speak His Word.

I love this declaration personalised from Romans 12:12: I am joyful in hope, patient in affliction, faithful in prayer. What a wonderful confession. It is such a beautiful scripture to speak over your life and even the lives of your loved ones. Maybe these things don't feel true right now. Perhaps you are neither joyful nor hopeful. Life might feel quite chaotic and hopeless. Maybe you are not even faithful in prayer and you don't have the patience to think about your impatience.

Being bolder means you can pray scriptures that speak what you want to see and not the circumstances before you. You have the courage to open your mouth and create your world with your words. You can call forth those things that are not as though they are with faith and watch your life change with the word of God.

If you take the time to pray this scripture over your life often, it will not only fill you with boldness, and hope, and renew your mind, it will become true. When challenging things arise, you will be joyful in hope and patient even in affliction because you know God is working it out. And as you wait, you'll pray faithfully and draw strength from communion with God. You will marvel at the word coming to life in your life.

There are so many other scriptures you can find, personalise, and speak. Search the Word of God for His promises and Spirit-filled confessions and declarations. Take time to find them, write them and speak them.

What do you say to yourself about yourself? How do you speak about your circumstances? From today, choose to speak life and truth.

I remember teaching at an event a few years ago. The scripture God gave me to teach encouraged and humbled me. It was a blessing and a warning.

"So, tell them, 'As surely as I live, declares the LORD, I will do to you the very thing I heard you say." Numbers 14:28 NIV

What can God hear you say? Think about this today.

praying scripture - 3

DAY 28

"And they praised God because of me." Galatians 1:24

Today's verse is a powerful scripture to pray over your life. It is short but incredibly impactful. Let me tell you why. In the preceding verses, Paul explains that though he was unknown, the testimony of what God had done in his life was so powerful that people who didn't know him had heard about him.

Galatians 1:23 says: "They only heard the report: The man who formerly persecuted us is now preaching the faith he once tried to destroy." Then he goes on to tell us in verse 24, "And they praise God because of me."

When you pray Galatians 1:24, you are declaring transformation into your life; the type that causes people to marvel and praise God. Your life can become such a testimony of the transformative power of God that people will glorify God because of you.

God is a story changer. He can cause a turnaround in your life. He wants to turn your present pain into a past situation so that men will look at you and praise Him. Your life will cause men to marvel and point, they will say isn't that:

- The one who was rejected?
- The one who was broke?
- The one who was sick?
- The one who was barren?
- The one who was homeless?
- The one who was insane?
- The one who was addicted?

With God, your story can become history. God wants to change your story today. Hallelujah!

Being bolder means you are not afraid to put God in remembrance of His word. The same God who did it for Paul will do it for you. He will take your past pain and turn it into present glory for His name's sake. He will change your story; he may even change your name. You will no longer be defined by negative circumstances but by words in line with the goodness of God. People will use their mouths to confirm the change in your story and say:

- The one who is accepted
- The one who is rich
- The one who is healed
- The one who is a mother
- The one who is a homeowner
- The one who has a sound mind
- The one who is free

When you pray this scripture over your life, you are declaring yourself as a testimony, a life that is willing to shine bright for others to see and give glory to God. We will praise God because of you.

praying scripture - 4

DAY 29

"Then you will know the truth, and the truth will set you free." John 8:32

At the beginning of this section on praying scriptures, I put a disclaimer which says: Some scriptures come with conditions that require us to act. Don't quote them blindly. If there's an action attached to the promise, then do it. Working the Word is a partnership; do your part and God will do His.

Today's verse allows me to explain what I mean. John 8:32 is a well-loved and well-used scripture. It is a word with a promise that we love, and I pray with it too. I say: "In the name of Jesus, according to Your word, I declare I will know the truth, and the truth will set me free."

I love this verse because when I pray it, I am trusting God to open my heart to the truth of His word so I receive wisdom, discernment, knowledge and understanding to live a life of freedom. I want to know the truth and be free. The devil is a liar. I refuse to live a life of bondage and deception, one that is limited by lies, when there is truth and freedom in Jesus. So, I declare this scripture over my life.

However, this is one of those scriptures that needs to be prayed in context because there is a condition attached to the promise and for you to claim the promise of liberating truth, you have to engage with the condition that leads to the fulfilment of the promise. That condition is found in the preceding verse.

John 8:31(ESV) says: "So Jesus said to the Jews who had believed him, 'If you abide in my word, you are truly my disciples.'"

As you can see from verse 31, abiding in God's Word is an important prerequisite for the fulfilment of the promise. So, if you pray John 8:32 only, personalising and quoting it continuously every day without doing John 8:31 then you will be praying amiss.

You must abide first. Abiding in His word will make you more like Jesus. You learn so much truth in the Word that it leads you to freedom. Jesus has promised if you abide in His Word, you will become His disciple and you will know the truth and the truth will set you free. Jesus himself is the truth. The Bible reveals this to us in John 14:6a: "Jesus answered, 'I am the way and the truth and the life...'" We also learn from scripture that Jesus is the word (John 1:1), so to have the truth that sets us free, we need to truly abide in Jesus because in Him is freedom. You cannot pray John 8:32 without doing John 8:31 and expect to see the manifestation of the Word.

I hope this gives you a good understanding of the importance of praying scripture correctly so you pray scripture in context, noting those scriptures that require a prerequisite action and taking the right actions to receive the promise of the Word of God. I also ask you to continue to be sensitive to the correction of the Holy Spirit. God is kind; He does not leave us in error, even when we pray scripture amiss and try to put God in remembrance of His Word, He will find ways to put us in remembrance of the conditions. Today's message might be one of those ways for you.

Take a moment now to think of all the scriptures you have been praying over your life and check if there are actions you need to do as well. Remember, you have the Holy Spirit who is a guide and helper. Ask Him to help you do those things which in your strength you cannot do. For example, considering taking today's verse, you can ask Him for the discipline to abide.

the praying scripture alarm - 5

DAY 30

If I were to rank the chapters of the Bible I think all Christians should memorise, Psalm 23 would be in my top ten. I absolutely love and enjoy praying this chapter.

My love for this psalm is for good reason. Very few chapters of the Bible pack as much power into so few verses as this chapter does. There are promises, provisions, directions, security, comfort, salvation, restoration, etc. We often quote the last verse of Psalm 23 when we share the grace in fellowship, but there is so much important stuff in verses 1-5 that we can pray with. I was away with my dear friend for a weekend recently and didn't realise she had noticed me pause and pray ever so often (I did try to hide it) until she asked me what I was doing. I shared the method I am going to teach you today with her, and she loved it. Since then, she has embraced it. She now often reminds me we are synced when we pray Psalm 23. Seeing how much she has enjoyed and been blessed by this method, I'm persuaded to share it with you. I call it the Praying Scripture Alarm. It's a simple but effective way to cultivate the art of proactive and consistent scripture prayer.

HOW TO SET UP A PRAYING SCRIPTURE ALARM

For this method, you will need a phone or a device that enables you to set a recurring alarm. Then follow these steps:

1. Choose a scripture (Chapter or Verse). I recommend Psalm 23, but you can ask the Holy Spirit to guide you.
2. Choose a frequency for your prayer. I recommend 3 or 6-hour blocks i.e., 6 am, 9 am, 12 pm, etc. Make sure you choose carefully, considering your lifestyle and what you can commit to. Start slowly and increase or decrease your frequency.
3. Set up the alarm on your device and title it Praying Scripture Alarm or the Verse you have chosen to Pause and Pray. You can set this up daily or pick a day or more in the week. If you are new to having a prayer schedule, I suggest you start with twice a day one day a week i.e., 12 p.m. and 6 p.m., and build up by adding more days.
4. Each time the alarm goes off, simply pause and pray the scripture over your life. It will be quick; Psalm 23 takes 60 seconds to read.

HELPFUL TIPS

- Stick to the same chapter or verse for an extended period as it will help you memorise it and embed it into your subconscious. It's a marathon, not a sprint.
- Don't be hard on yourself if you miss an alarm. Just pray as soon as you can. This is a guide; it should be

fun, not punishment. However, try as much as you can to be consistent. It can help you build prayer discipline.
- Vary the versions of the bible passage you read to keep it interesting and give you a fuller understanding of the word. I love the KJV, but NIV and NLT are great versions too. Don't stick to your default Bible version; try others. It truly enriches the experience.
- Get a Praying Scripture buddy. Being accountable to someone on a similar journey can make the process more enjoyable. You can do this as a small group or as a church.

I hope you try this out. It only takes a minute or two and can be quite rewarding.

PS: The Praying Scripture Alarm is an aid for your scripture prayer life and should not become a burdensome religious observance. If you miss an alarm or a day, it's absolutely fine. Don't let the enemy use this tool to bring condemnation or guilt into your life. That's not of God and not the purpose of the alarm. I don't always pray when my alarm goes off because life happens. I do however try to pray as soon as I can. Please do not put yourself under any religious burden and suck the life out of a habit that should bring you joy.

Also, continue to read or pray other scriptures at other times of the day. This method should not replace your daily devotion or Bible study. I hope it enriches your prayer life.

praying prayers from the bible - 6

DAY 31

Yesterday, I shared with you a simple method for praying scripture consistently and building up your faith. Today, I want to teach you about praying prayers from the Bible. From the Old to the New Testament, there are numerous examples of men and women who prayed and God answered. We can pray their prayers.

Life can be challenging, and we often encounter obstacles that leave us speechless. How do you pray when you don't have the words to pray? The good news is, there are no new situations. Even in the hardest circumstances, we can find examples of people in the Bible who faced those adversities and overcame them. Some of those people even left prayers for us that we can use. Take some time to read Acts 4 which tells us the story of Peter and John. They were preaching the message of Jesus which the religious leaders didn't like at all. So, they had them arrested, jailed, and flogged before eventually releasing them. They warned them never to speak or teach the name of Jesus. Despite this warning, they went back to the other disciples, told them all that happened, and then together, the believers prayed a beautiful and powerful prayer for boldness. See Acts 4:24-31. You too can pray this prayer aloud, asking God to make you bolder. He will fill you with the courage you need to step out and proclaim His word and to live your life with purpose.

Do you need wisdom, faith, courage, children, increase, protection, health etc.? There are scriptures with prayers that will speak to your circumstances. Find them and pray them.

Here are some more prayers in the Bible:

- Moses - Psalm 90
- Hannah - 1 Samuel 2:1-10
- Jonah - Jonah 2:1-9
- Solomon - 1 Kings 8:22-53
- Jesus - Matthew 6:9-13
- Paul - Ephesians 1:16-19

The Bible is rich with prayers. Take the time to pray them.

I have personalised the Prayer of Jabez from 1 Chronicles 4:10: “Amanda cried out to the God of Israel, 'Oh, that you would bless me and enlarge my territory! Let your hand be with me and keep me from harm so that I will be free from pain.' And God granted my request.”

Isn’t this a wonderful prayer? It's the kind of prayer you don’t need to add to or remove from. Just put your name in it and pray it over your life. I love this prayer; it is complete and impactful.

I am thankful God’s word is true, so I can pray it with faith and thanksgiving, knowing, like the last line above states, GOD GRANTED MY REQUEST. I believe He has because my

Bible tells me He did this for Jabez. He is the same God. If He did it for Jabez, He will do it for me and you. God wants to grant your request today. I encourage you to put your name in that prayer and start to speak it over your life, and pray it consistently.

Another example is found in 3 John 1:2. Personalise it by saying, "I pray I may enjoy good health and all may go well with me, even as my soul is getting along well." You can also declare the verse over someone in your world who is sick: "Dear friend, I pray you may enjoy good health and all may go well with you, even as your soul is getting along well."

Use the Word of God to bring change in your life and the lives of others. There are many prayers in the Bible. Find them and pray them. When you pray prayers from the Bible, the hand of God moves over your life according to His will.

end note

Congratulations on completing this 31-day Bolder journey. I know God has done something amazing in your life. I am confident in this not because of any wisdom on my part, but because you have encountered the Word of God, which is a catalyst for healing and transformation. Praise God!

Welcome to a bolder version of you. Shine bright, walk tall, and step out in faith, knowing God has you always. Like the psalmist said, "God is within her, she will not fall; God will help her at break of day." Psalm 46:5. You are loved and helped by God.

If you have enjoyed this devotional, why not gift one to a loved one? Be a blessing to the girls and women in your life by sharing copies of this devotional with them. They will thank God for it and praise Him because of you.

other books by amanda bedzrah

Fiction

- Becoming Queen Bathsheba
- Leah: Unnoticed. Unwanted. Unloved

Non – Fiction

- The Love that set me free
- Overcoming the fear of death
- Praying Proverbs
- 5 Habits of Godly Resilient Women
- My Super Power is Kindness (A Journal for Kids)
- Choosing Kindness Everyday (A Journal for Teenage Girls & Women)

about the author

ABOUT THE AUTHOR

Reverend Amanda is a wife and a mother to three beautiful children. She is passionate about seeing people restored and living a full life beyond salvation. She is a passionate Bible teacher who believes in the transformative power of God's word, teaching with practical examples and bringing the Bible to life. She is a Prayer Minister, an Inspirational Speaker and Mentor.

Reverend Amanda is also an award-winning author, with much of her work grounded in the redeeming, empowering and transformative power of God's love. Her debut book, The Love That Set Me Free was met with critical acclaim, with readers recognising themselves and finding healing through her autobiographical account of childhood abuse, suppression and trauma. Since then, she has authored several instructional guides for living life fully according to God's will both fiction and non-fiction books.

Reverend Amanda is a Senior NHS Professional, working as the Associate Director for Immunisation and Vaccinations NHS Kent and Medway ICB in the UK. Amanda is a Law Graduate (LLb Hons), a Prince 2 Practitioner, she is certified in Business Analysis Practice and holds several leadership qualifications and continues to pursue deeper study of the word with various training and courses.

She is the founder and CEO of Empower a Woman (EAW), a UK based non-profit organisation that is set up to meet the needs of vulnerable women.

For more information about please visit her websites:

www.amandabedzrah.com
www.empowerawoman.org

facebook.com/amandabedzrah
instagram.com/Amanda_Bedzrah

Printed in Great Britain
by Amazon

35550211R00076